DIGITAL CITIZENS

MY DIGITAL RIGHTS AND RULES

BEN HUBBARD
ILLUSTRATED BY DIEGO VAISBERG

Lerner Publications ◆ Minneapolis

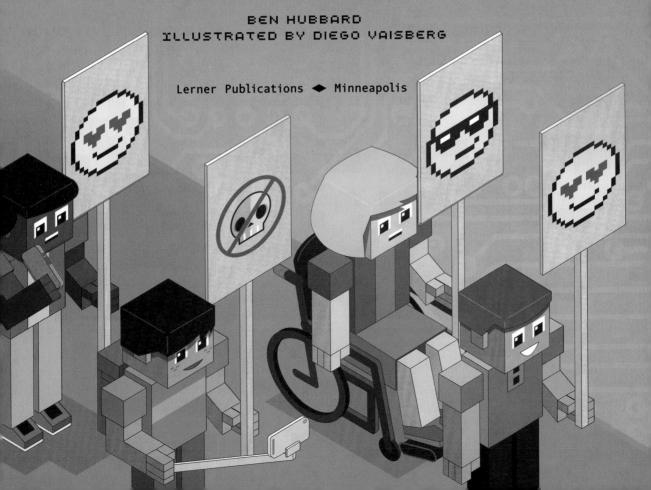

First American edition published in 2019 by Lerner
Publishing Group, Inc.

First published in Great Britain in 2018 by
The Watts Publishing Group
Copyright © The Watts Publishing
Group 2018

Credits
Series Editor: Julia Bird
Illustrator: Diego Vaisberg
Packaged by: Collaborate

Lerner Publications Company
A division of Lerner Publishing Group, Inc.
241 First Avenue North
Minneapolis, MN 55401 USA

For reading levels and more information, look up
this title at www.lernerbooks.com.

Main body text set in Courier PS Std.
Typeface provided by Monotype Typography.

Library of Congress Cataloging-in-Publication Data

Names: Hubbard, Ben C., author. | Vaisberg, Diego, illustrator.
Title: My digital rights and rules / Ben Hubbard, Diego Vaisberg.
Description: Minneapolis : Lerner Publications, 2018. | Series:
Digital citizens | Includes bibliographical references and index.
Identifiers: LCCN 2018026998 (print) | LCCN 2018030667 (ebook) |
ISBN 9781541543089 (eb pdf) | ISBN 9781541538818 (lb : alk. paper)
Subjects: LCSH: Information technology—Law and legislation—United
States—Juvenile literature. | Internet—Law and legislation—United
States—Juvenile literature. | Privacy, Right of—United States—
Juvenile literature. | Copyright and electronic data processing—
United States—Juvenile literature. | Digital rights management—United
States—Juvenile literature. | Data protection—Law and legislation—
United States—Juvenile literature.
Classification: LCC KF390.5.C6 (ebook) | LCC KF390.5.C6 H83 2018
(print) | DDC 343.7309/944—dc23

LC record available at https://lccn.loc.gov/2018026998

Manufactured in the United States of America
1-45064-35891-7/16/2018

CONTENTS

WHAT IS DIGITAL CITIZENSHIP?

When we log onto the internet, we become part of a giant online world.

In this world we can use our smartphones, tablets, and computers to explore, create, and communicate with billions of different people. Together, these people make up a global digital community. That is why they are known as digital citizens. When you use the internet you are a digital citizen too. So what does this mean?

CITIZEN VS. DIGITAL CITIZEN

A good citizen is someone who behaves well, looks after themselves and others, and tries to make their community a better place. A good digital citizen acts exactly the same way. However, the online world is bigger than just a local neighborhood, city, or country. It spans the whole world and crosses every kind of border. It is therefore up to all digital citizens everywhere to make this digital community a safe, fun, and exciting place for everyone.

RULES ARE BORING. WHY DO WE HAVE THEM?

OFTEN THEY ARE THERE TO PROTECT YOU.

IS IT MY RIGHT TO BAN MY BROTHER FROM USING MY TABLET?

UMM . . .

MY DIGITAL RIGHTS AND RULES

Citizens that behave well and follow the rules of their community have certain rights. A right is something a person is entitled to as a human being, such as food, shelter, or protection from harm. Rights also give people certain privileges, such as free speech. This book is all about your online rights, as well as some rules you should follow to be a good digital citizen.

KNOW YOUR RIGHTS

In today's world, everyone should have the right to become a digital citizen with access to the internet.

As digital citizens, we also have certain rights when we go online. But to keep these rights we need to behave responsibly and play by the rules. So what are a digital citizen's rights, rules, and responsibilities?

RULES

Sometimes it can seem like the internet has no rules. But it actually has many of the same rules as the real world. For example, it is against the rules to bully others or tell lies about them. It is also against the rules to steal other people's work or download things illegally (see pages 22–23). Your school or parents may have some of their own rules about how you use the internet too.

SARAH SAYS YOU POSTED A RUDE COMMENT ABOUT HER SHOES.

RESPONSIBILITIES

Being a responsible digital citizen means behaving in the same way you would in the real world. That means respecting others, being polite, protecting yourself and people you know, and helping others when you can.

WHAT ARE YOU DOING?

EXERCISING MY RIGHT TO FREE SPEECH.

WERE YOU USING YOUR PHONE DURING CLASS TODAY?

BUT FOOTBALL PRACTICE STARTED 10 MINUTES AGO.

RIGHTS

Just like in the real world, you have the right to be safe, protected, and free from abuse while online. You also have the right to privacy, free speech, and the right to search freely for information. However, access to some websites may be against the rules of your school, parents, or country.

RULE OF THE TOOLS

For many people, having a digital device that is constantly connected to the internet seems like a normal part of everyday life.

But we should never take these for granted and remember that they are tools, not toys. For this reason, it's important to take care of your digital devices and use them responsibly. This means switching them off in places you're not supposed to use them.

PHONE HOME

Your parents may have some rules about when you can use your phone, tablet, or computer and for how long. It doesn't always feel like it, but these rules are often there for your own good. It's also fair that your parents set these rules. After all, they are usually the ones paying for you to be online!

SCHOOL RULES

Your school may also have rules about when you can use your digital device. Often they are in place so you pay attention in class and don't disrupt others. Good digital citizens respect the rules and use their common sense about using their digital devices outside of the classroom too. Talking loudly or playing music on smartphones is not a good way to behave in libraries or on public transit.

DEVICE WATCH

With so much of our personal information on our smartphones, it is important to take extra care of them. Most of all, this means never leaving them unattended in public. After all, a phone is an easy thing to snatch.

INFORMATION INVASION

The internet is a free resource, and we should all have the freedom to seek and receive information from it.

However, sometimes websites that are harmful or inappropriate for children are blocked. You can ask a teacher or parent to explain why you have been blocked from using certain websites. Digital citizens should be allowed to ask about online rules so they can understand why they are obeying them.

WHY CAN'T I OPEN THE NASA WEBSITE TODAY?

AND I CAN'T VISIT NATIONAL GEOGRAPHIC ANYMORE!

FILTERS

Internet filters are put in place to block websites with particular content, such as violence. These websites aren't good for children and can be confusing or upsetting. However, sometimes filters also block helpful websites by mistake. If you think something has been blocked incorrectly, point it out to a parent or teacher.

WHICH WEBSITES ARE HARMFUL?

Websites that are definitely harmful are those that promote hatred or violence toward others. Websites with adult themes are also not appropriate for children. Websites that ask for your personal information should always be avoided. However, a simple rule of thumb is, if you see anything that you don't like on a website, just click out.

EXCUSE ME, SIR. WE CAN'T ACCESS OUR FAVORITE SITES.

OUR NEW CONTENT FILTERS MUST HAVE BLOCKED THEM BY ACCIDENT. I'LL GET THIS FIXED.

FREE SPEECH

Free speech is one of any citizen's central rights, including digital citizens.

This means not being scared to say what you think when you post a comment, message, or blog online. However, it doesn't mean being able to say anything at all. In the online world people need to respect others and their opinions, even if they disagree with them.

WHAT IS FREE SPEECH?

Free speech is a recognized human right according to international law. It gives people the right to express themselves without interference. This important right was partly won during the eighteenth-century French and American revolutions, when people rose up against their rulers.

FREE SPEECH GONE BAD

Freedom of speech is not covered by law when people say rude or hurtful things about others. This is especially true when attacks are made against people because of their skin color, religion, or country of origin. These are known as hate crimes and are taken very seriously by the police.

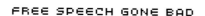

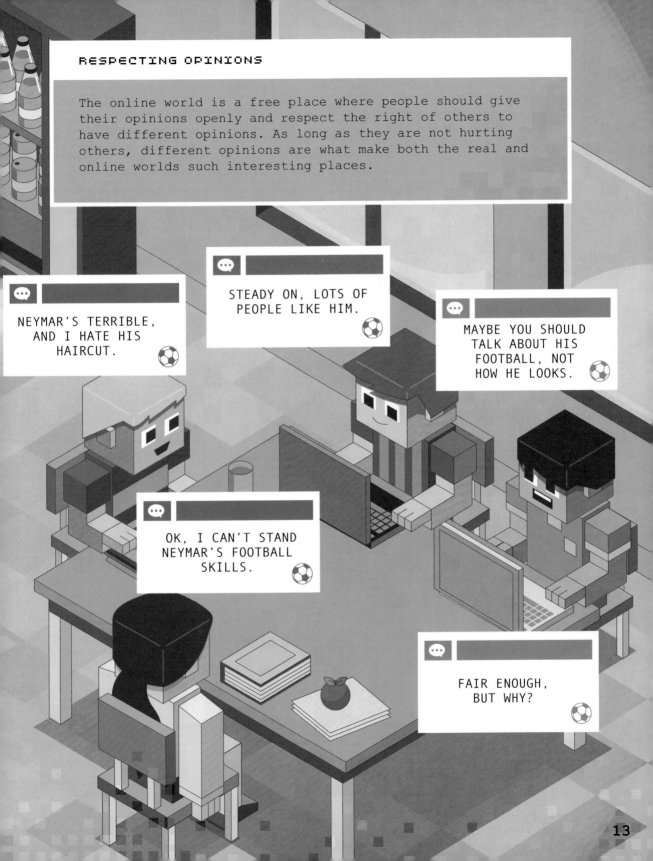

RESPECTING OPINIONS

The online world is a free place where people should give their opinions openly and respect the right of others to have different opinions. As long as they are not hurting others, different opinions are what make both the real and online worlds such interesting places.

STEADY ON, LOTS OF PEOPLE LIKE HIM.

NEYMAR'S TERRIBLE, AND I HATE HIS HAIRCUT.

MAYBE YOU SHOULD TALK ABOUT HIS FOOTBALL, NOT HOW HE LOOKS.

OK, I CAN'T STAND NEYMAR'S FOOTBALL SKILLS.

FAIR ENOUGH, BUT WHY?

PROTECTING OTHERS, PROTECTING YOURSELF

In the online world we have to look after ourselves and the people around us.

That means protecting them from things that could be harmful or upsetting. It's easy to share or write things on social media or post photos to our accounts. But if not checked first, these can sometimes have consequences later on.

THAT'S GREAT, I'M POSTING IT RIGHT AWAY.

PERSONAL INFORMATION

Your personal information is made up of your private details: your age, name, school, telephone number, and address. These are things you need to protect when you are online, so strangers can't find out too much about you. You need to protect the details of your friends and family too.

REVEALING PHOTOS

Have you ever heard the saying "One picture is worth a thousand words"? This can be true of photos you post online. Often these can give away too much personal information about yourself or your friends—such as where they live or go to school. Make sure to check a photo before you post it.

LOOK, THE PHOTO SHOWS HENRY'S HOUSE NUMBER AND STREET NAME.

YOU'RE RIGHT, IT'S GIVING TOO MUCH OF HENRY'S INFORMATION AWAY. I'LL TAKE A DIFFERENT SHOT.

HURTFUL COMMENTS

Good digital citizens report and delete nasty messages, emails, or texts and never spread them around. If someone has said something hurtful about someone you know online, it's your responsibility not to forward it on.

PRIVACY PARTICULARS

Many of us use social media accounts to keep in touch with friends and family.

When we post information such as photos or blogs we assume it will stay only on the social media website. But how can we be sure? Sometimes we might find our posts and photos appearing elsewhere on the internet.

I LOOK SO GROWN-UP, I CAN'T WAIT FOR EVERYONE TO SEE MY PHOTO.

PRIVACY POLICY

Every social media website has its own rules about how your information is used. It is up to you to check you are happy with a website's privacy policy and that your information will be protected from being shown elsewhere. The easiest way is to ask a trusted adult to help you read a social media site's privacy policy before joining it.

SOCIAL SETTINGS

The privacy settings on your social media account allow you to choose who looks at what you post. Choosing "only friends" is the best setting. You can often also adjust the settings so only a selected group of your friends can see your photos, posts, or other private information.

LOOK, MY PHOTO IS ALL OVER THE PLACE. I DIDN'T AGREE TO THIS.

I THINK YOU'VE FORGOTTEN TO SET THE CORRECT PRIVACY SETTINGS ON YOUR SOCIAL MEDIA ACCOUNT.

INFORMATION ASTRAY

Making sure our information is protected on our social media accounts is important. But once we post something online, we no longer have complete control over it. Photos are easy to copy and post elsewhere, and there is always a risk your account will be hacked. This is why it's important to be happy with the things you post.

DIGITAL LAW

Digital law is designed to protect digital citizens against online crime.

Online crime can include identity theft, illegal downloading, and bullying. However, every country has different laws about online crime, and there is no international police force looking after the internet. That is why if you see something you think is harmful or wrong, it is always a good idea to report it to a trusted adult.

HARASSMENT AND BULLYING

While many countries agree that online bullying is a crime, not all agree on what should be done about it. When online bullying happens among children, often the local police work in conjunction with the school. Those found guilty can be expelled from the school or prosecuted under harassment laws. The simplest thing to do is tell a trusted adult if it is happening to you or someone you know.

EWWW! SOMEONE HAS PUT HORRIBLE PICTURES ALL OVER MY WALL.

COME ON, LET'S TELL MY DAD.

 ### WHAT ARE ONLINE CRIMES?

The following are typical online crimes:

1 Hacking into websites

2 Stealing someone's information or identity

3 Illegal file sharing

DEFAMATION

Telling lies about someone is a crime known as defamation. Defamation can be something that is written, known as libel, or something that is spoken, known as slander. Defamation is very serious if somebody tells lies that damage a person's reputation. If someone is found guilty of this crime, they often have to pay a lot of money to the person they defamed.

THANKS FOR SHOWING ME. I'M GOING TO CONTACT YOUR SCHOOL AND THEN THE POLICE.

4 Plagiarizing people's work (see pages 20-21)

5 Creating viruses

6 Pirating software

ORIGINAL ONLINE WORK

Can you imagine if you wrote an essay, article, or book that somebody then claimed was their work?

This is what it is like for people who have their work plagiarized. Under copyright law, it is illegal to pretend to have created something that you have not. This includes using someone else's writing for school essays and homework.

JULIE, I NEED TO SEE YOU ABOUT YOUR ASSIGNMENT.

CITING SOURCES

Often when we are doing research we find a writer has summed up something so well that we wish we had written it ourselves. It's okay to use a writer's exact words if you get permission to do so and then attribute the text to them. This is called "citing your sources." You can ask your teacher how to cite sources in your homework and essays.

ESSAYS AND HOMEWORK

It's easy to cut and paste a sentence from a webpage and then drop it into your own essay or homework assignment. It may not seem serious, but doing so is plagiarizing someone else's work. In serious cases, students have handed in whole essays that they have copied directly from the internet. It's not difficult to find out if something has been plagiarized, and it can get that person into a lot of trouble.

I REALLY LIKED YOUR ESSAY, BUT THERE WERE SOME SENTENCES THAT YOU PASTED STRAIGHT FROM THE INTERNET.

I THOUGHT ONE SENTENCE HERE AND THERE WAS OK.

IT WOULD BE IF YOU ATTRIBUTED THE SENTENCES TO THE ORIGINAL AUTHOR. LET ME SHOW YOU HOW TO DO THAT.

ILLEGAL DOWNLOADS

It might seem like lots of people download music, films, and games for free these days.

However, downloading any material that is under copyright is stealing and is therefore against the law. Copyright law applies to everyone, no matter what age they are. That means anyone that illegally downloads files could get into trouble.

LOOK, EVEN THE NEW LEGO MOVIE IS ON HERE.

YOU'RE SURE WE WON'T GET INTO TROUBLE?

AWESOME, I'M GETTING IT TONIGHT.

I DON'T KNOW, IT SEEMS DODGY.

WHAT IS COPYRIGHT?

When somebody creates something, such as a book, song, or film, they own it under copyright. This means they get to decide what happens to it. To use the work, people normally have to seek the copyright-holder's permission and pay a fee. This stops people stealing the work of others. It also means if you download something that is under copyright for free, you are breaking the law.

ILLEGAL DOWNLOADING

There are many legal websites where you can pay a fee to download films, songs, or books. Then there are other illegal websites that offer these files for free. By using these sites, people are not only breaking the law but also run the risk of downloading a file that contains harmful malware or viruses. Often the quality of these files can also be very poor. It is best to avoid these websites and this file-sharing altogether, even if it is tempting to get something for nothing.

I DOWNLOADED THAT MOVIE, BUT THE SOUND IS TERRIBLE.

PHEW! GLAD I DIDN'T JOIN IN.

AND MY LAPTOP STARTED ACTING WEIRDLY AFTERWARD.

YEAH, ME TOO. I'M SORRY.

ACCESS FOR ALL

Today, digital technology is all around us.
We use this technology to learn, have fun, and message our friends. Surely everyone in the world must own at least one digital device, such as a laptop, tablet, or smartphone—right? That's not actually the case. In many places, children don't own any digital devices. Others don't have access to the internet at all.

YOUR TURN IN 15 MINUTES.

A WORLD OF OPPORTUNITY

Good digital citizens believe that everyone should have online access, regardless of who they are, where they live, and how much money they have. No one should miss out on the amazing opportunities the online world can offer.

HOW CAN I HELP?

There are lots of ways you can help bring internet access to those without it, both in your own community and beyond. Here are a few of them:

RECYCLE OLD DEVICES

Ask your teacher if your school can set up a recycling box for old, unwanted digital devices. These phones, tablets, and computers can go to less fortunate people in your area or abroad.

FUNDRAISERS FOR FACILITIES

Holding a fundraiser, such as a bake sale, can help your school buy digital devices for your school library or computer room or to lend out to students. Ask your teacher about organizing one.

DID YOU KNOW ONLY AROUND HALF THE PEOPLE ON EARTH HAVE INTERNET ACCESS?

BAKE SALE TODAY

FOR SALE

DID YOU KNOW ONLY AROUND 30 PERCENT OF PEOPLE ON EARTH OWN A SMARTPHONE?

ASK YOUR PARENTS

Adults can be helpful sometimes because they know lots of other adults. Ask your parents if they know any businesses that would donate money or digital devices to your school. They might be happy to help when they find out what you're doing.

HELP EVERYONE PARTICIPATE

Helping others participate in the online world can often begin close to home.

There are always people around us who don't have the latest phone or tablet. There are many others who can't use their digital devices properly! Good digital citizens try to involve and educate those around them, so everybody can keep up with the latest trends and technologies.

INCLUDING EVERYONE

It's easy for those without a digital device or internet connection to feel left out. But you can include them by showing them the latest applications on yours. After all, we all need help learning new things from time to time.

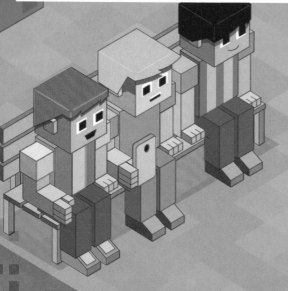

COME AND HAVE A LOOK AT HOW THIS NEW MESSAGING APP WORKS.

SPECIAL NEEDS

Some students with special needs can struggle using digital devices. They may not be able to see them well, or they may find it hard to hold them. Schools should always make sure these students are getting the same access as everyone else. If you see they are not, talk to your teacher about helping them.

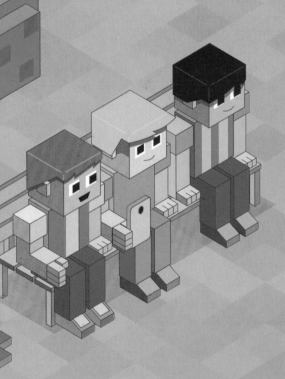

THIS IS HOW YOU SEND A MESSAGE.

HOW DO YOU INVITE FRIENDS TO JOIN?

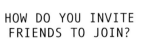 DIGITAL DIVIDE

The Digital Divide refers to the gap between those who have digital access and those who don't. With the spread of smartphones, more people have access to the internet than ever before. But there is still a long way to go before everyone can be a digital citizen.

DIGITAL QUIZ

Now you've reached the end of this book how do you feel about your digital rights and rules? How much have you learned? And how much can you remember? Take this quiz and tally up your score at the end to find out.

1. Which of these is a digital right?
a. To be given a free smartphone
b. Freedom of speech
c. Freedom to say anything to anyone

2. The gap between those who do and do not have intent access is called:
a. The Internet Interval
b. The Online Opening
c. The Digital Divide

3. Where should you not use your smartphone?
a. At the beach
b. In class
c. At the park

4. When is it OK to use an author's work from online?
a. When you cite your sources
b. When you change all the letters into capitals
c. By taking out all the apostrophes

5. What privacy setting should you use on your social media account?
a. Only my friends
b. Friends of friends
c. Everyone

6. Which of these is a form of defamation?
a. Tribal
b. Libel
.c. Mabel

7. Which of these is not an example of your personal information?
a. Your avatar
b. Your real name
c. Your address

8. Which of these is not an online crime?
a. Hacking into websites
b. Calling someone stupid in a blog
c. Stealing someone's identity

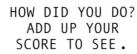

HOW DID YOU DO? ADD UP YOUR SCORE TO SEE.

1-4: You are on your way, but retake the quiz to get a score over 4.

5-7: You've passed the quiz well. Now see if you can pass the quiz in the book *My Digital Future.*

8: Wow! 8 out of 8. You are a natural born digital citizen

ANSWERS

1: b; 2: c; 3: b; 4: a; 5: a; 6: b; 7: a; 8: b

GLOSSARY

avatar
A computer icon or image that people use to represent themselves online

block
A way of stopping someone from sending you nasty messages, or being stopped from entering a website

digital
Technology that involves computers

download
To take information or files from the internet and store them on your computer

hack
To break into computers and computer networks online

internet
The vast electronic network that allows billions of computers from around the world to connect to each other

malware
A dangerous computer program that is created to damage or disable other digital devices

online
Being connected to the internet by using a computer or digital device

privacy settings
Controls on social media websites that allow you to decide who has access to your profile and posts

search engine
A computer program that carries out a search of available information on the internet based on the words you type in

smartphone
A mobile phone that is capable of connecting to the internet

social media
Websites that allow users to share content and information online

trusted adult
An adult you know well and trust who can help you with all issues relating to the internet

virus
A dangerous program that can "infect" a computer, destroying the information it holds

website
A collection of web pages that is stored on a computer and made available to people over the internet

HELPFUL WEBSITES

Digital Citizenship
The following websites have helpful information about digital citizenship for young people:

http://www.digizen.org/kids/

http://www.digitalcitizenship.nsw.edu.au/Prim_Splash/

http://www.cyberwise.org/digital-citizenship-games

Bullying
These websites have excellent advice for kids who are experiencing bullying online:

https://www.childline.org.uk/info-advice/bullying-abuse-safety/types-bullying/online-bullying

http://www.bullying.co.uk

https://www.stopbullying.gov/kids/facts/

Staying Safe
These websites are dedicated to keeping kids safe online, with lots of good advice:

http://www.childnet.com/young-people/primary

http://www.kidsmart.org.uk

http://www.safetynetkids.org.uk/personal-safety/staying-safe-online/

http://www.bbc.co.uk/newsround/13910067

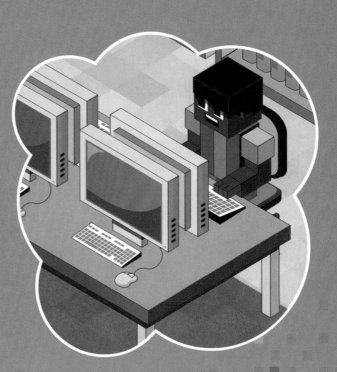

INDEX

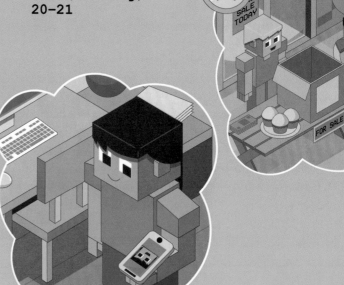

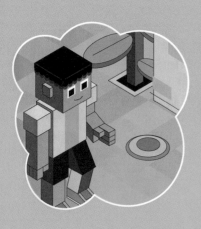

Understanding Charts and Graphs

New Hanover County Public Library
201 Chestnut Street
Wilmington, North Carolina 28401

CHRISTINE TAYLOR-BUTLER

Children's Press®
An Imprint of Scholastic Inc.
New York Toronto London Auckland Sydney
Mexico City New Delhi Hong Kong
Danbury, Connecticut

Content Consultant
Nabil Al-Najjar, PhD
Professor and Chair, Managerial Economics & Decision Making Sciences Department
Kellogg School of Management
Northwestern University
Evanston, Illinois

Library of Congress Cataloging-in-Publication Data

Taylor-Butler, Christine.
  Understanding charts and graphs/by Christine Taylor-Butler.
    p. cm.—(A true book)
  Includes bibliographical references and index.
  ISBN 978-0-531-26009-8 (lib. bdg.) — ISBN 978-0-531-26240-5 (pbk.)
  1. Mathematical statistics—Juvenile literature. 2. Mathematics—Graphic methods—Juvenile lit-
erature. I. Title.
  QA273.16.T39 2012
  001.4'226—dc23   2012002643

All rights reserved. Published in 2013 by Children's Press, an imprint of Scholastic Inc.
Printed in China 62
SCHOLASTIC, CHILDREN'S PRESS, A TRUE BOOK™, and associated logos are trademarks and/or registered trademarks of Scholastic Inc.
1 2 3 4 5 6 7 8 9 10 R 22 21 20 19 18 17 16 15 14 13

Front cover: Pie chart, bar graph, and line graph
Back cover: Weather map

Find the Truth!

Everything you are about to read is true *except* for one of the sentences on this page.

Which one is **TRUE**?

T or F   Spreadsheets were tablecloths used by tax collectors to count the king's money.

T or F   The oldest known Mayan calendar dates as far as 7012 CE.

Find the answers in this book.

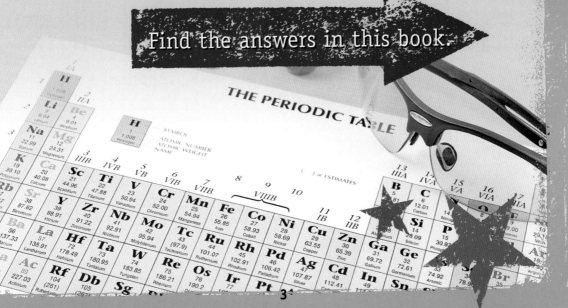

THE PERIODIC TABLE

3

Contents

THE BIG TRUTH!

March Madness

3 Graph It Out!

6%

13%

75%

4 Charts

Charts and graphs help organize complex infromation.

How can words, numbers, and pictures help organize information? **35**

Ancient Mayans carved calendars in stone and painted them on walls.

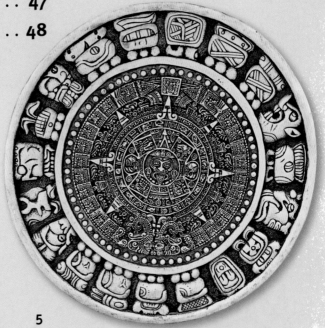

CHAPTER 1

Don't Say It– Show It!

Imagine visiting a restaurant. The waitress describes 100 meals the chef can prepare. Can you remember all the choices? How do you choose what to eat?

You ask for a menu. The menu is divided into groups: appetizers, soups and salads, main courses, desserts, and drinks. Does that make it easier to choose? It probably does. A menu is one example of a chart.

 The largest restaurant in the world has 6,014 seats.

Graphic Organizers

People come across charts, tables, and graphs in everyday life. Calendars keep track of important dates. Doctors record your health information on a medical chart. Engineers use flowcharts and graphs to plan large projects. Teachers use charts to show student progress and to record grades. Artists and writers use charts to brainstorm new ideas. Musicians use charts when they read sheet music. Another name for a chart, table, or graph is *graphic organizer*.

Doctors and nurses use graphic organizers to help them keep track of important patient information.

Calendars helped the Maya keep track of religious celebrations and other events.

The earliest graphic organizers date back thousands of years. Stone carvings of game boards appear in ancient Egyptian temples. The Mayan civilization created calendars that counted as far out as the year 7012 CE. Mathematicians and philosophers have used charts to teach logic problems for thousands of years.

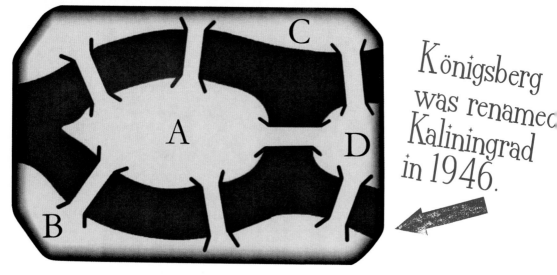

Leonhard Euler's map of bridge paths was one of the first modern graphs.

Inventive Organizers

In 1736, Swiss mathematician Leonhard Euler came up with the first modern ideas about graphs. He looked at the seven bridges that crossed a river running through the city of Königsberg, in present-day Russia. He wanted to prove that it was impossible to find a single path around the city that would cross each bridge only once. He used a series of **nodes** and lines to show the possible paths. An even number of bridges was needed to solve the problem.

In the 1780s, Scottish engineer William Playfair drew the first line and bar graphs. He used them to track goods being shipped between England and other countries. He thought a picture would be easier to understand than the columns of numbers normally used for this task. Playfair later drew circles with shaded sections to compare different areas of land. These circle graphs became the first known pie charts.

Pie charts are used often in modern business presentations.

11

The first digital table software, VisiCalc, was introduced in 1979. It became popular because it could sort data and perform math calculations quickly. Today, businesses use these tables, or spreadsheets, to look for trends and patterns. Scientists use them to make comparisons and draw conclusions from complicated data.

Spreadsheets help organize large amounts of data, making the information easier to analyze.

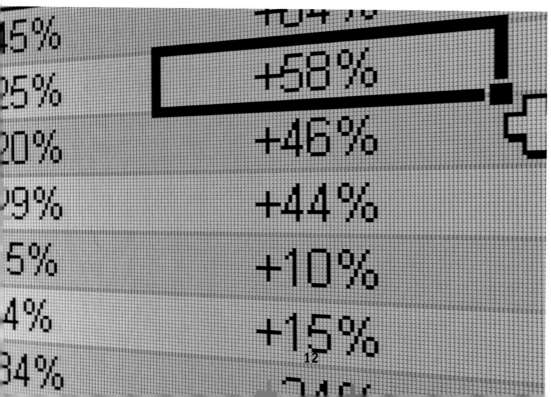

Spreadsheet programs are often used to turn data into other graphic organizers.

Spreadsheets can create more than one type of chart from the same data. The table of numbers is turned into pie charts, line graphs, and other graphic organizers so the data can be analyzed more easily. Presentation software such as PowerPoint makes it easy to share the information with large groups.

CHAPTER 2

Put It on the Table

Suppose you are visiting an airport. You want to know when your flight will leave. A monitor shows each airline, with each plane's flight number, time of departure, and gate where passengers will board. The chart is arranged as a table. The flight schedules are arranged in rows and columns, and are sorted by city or departure time. Tables make it easy to find information quickly.

 There are an estimated 28,000 airline flights each day in the United States.

Just the Facts

You probably use tables almost every day. A book's list of contents, an index, and even the ingredients on a box of cereal are examples of tables. You may also see tables in the classroom. A periodic table in your science class is one example. Students use addition, subtraction, multiplication, and division tables to learn math facts.

The periodic table is a necessary tool for learning about chemistry.

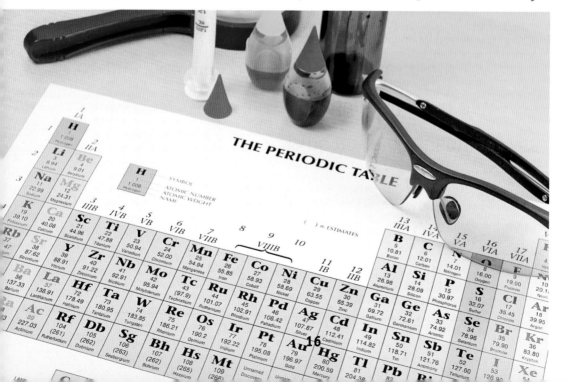

Try It!

You can make your own math fact sheet. Here's how:
1. On a sheet of notebook paper, copy the chart below.
2. Multiply the numbers of the column (1) to the row (1) that **intersect** at the first blank box at the top left corner of the chart. Place the answer in the box, as shown below.
3. Do the same for the other boxes, adding the numbers for the column and row that intersect at each box. Try timing yourself with a stopwatch or a clock with a second hand. How fast can you fill in the spaces?

Math fact sheets are good tools to use to practice for a test.

	1	2	3	4	5	6	7	8	9	10
1	1									
2										
3										
4										
5										
6										
7										
8										
9										
10										

Spreadsheets

Accountants and businesses use spreadsheets to keep track of money. Computer programs such as Excel can automatically add and subtract **credits** and **debits** when they are entered into the spreadsheet. This provides an up-to-date account balance, or total. Scientists who keep track of the results of experiments can use the program to calculate percentages and other information. The programs can also reorganize data according to date, size, or other guides.

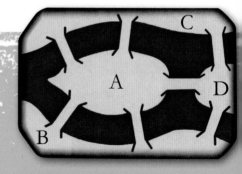

A Timeline of Charts and Graphs

1100s

Counting tables are used by King Henry II's treasurer to count taxes.

1736

Leonhard Euler writes the first paper describing graph theory.

Spreadsheets do not only deal in numbers. Words and phrases can be entered to organize people or events. Businesses and individuals can use spreadsheets to outline a schedule or track the progress of a project. Contact lists that include home addresses, phone numbers, and email addresses can be kept updated and alphabetized. People even use spreadsheet software to create to-do lists and checklists.

1801
William Playfair publishes *The Commercial and Political Atlas* and *The Statistical Breviary*, containing the first bar, line, and pie charts.

1858
French engineer Joseph Minard begins using pie charts in his work.

1979
Dan Bricklin and Bob Frankston invent VisiCalc, the first computer spreadsheet.

Personal Planners

A personal planner contains a calendar and a to-do list. Businesspeople use personal planners to help them remember the details of their schedules. Students throughout the world use planners to keep track of appointments, class times, homework assignments, and test dates.

The first 365-day calendar was introduced in ancient Egypt.

Planners are a great way to keep track of upcoming events.

Why Is It Called a Table?

Starting in the late 12th century, tax collectors in England set collected coins out on a table to count them. The edge of the table was four fingers high to keep the stacks of coins from falling off the edge. A tablecloth had rows and columns similar to a checkerboard. Each row and column held a specific value. The table was also used to count the king's money.

March Madness

Sports brackets keep track of winners and losers in a competition or event. The National Collegiate Athletic Association (NCAA) March Madness championship is one example. The tournament hosts 68 teams in the men's division and 64 teams in the women's division. The teams compete from March until April.

1 Teams are grouped into four regions. The regional teams are then paired for matches.

2 The winner of each match advances to the next round, in which they compete against the winner of another match.

3 The winners continue to advance on the chart until only one team remains.

4 The final winning team is declared the champion.

2012 NCAA March Madness Results

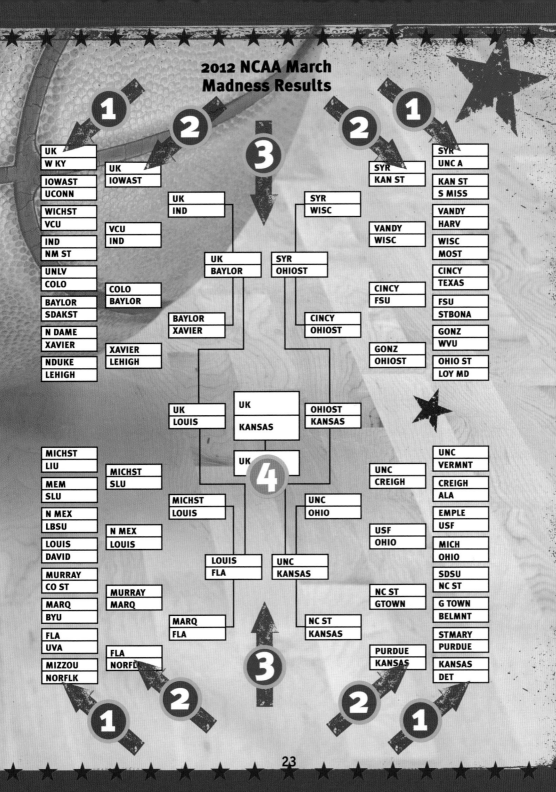

Dow Jones Industrial Average
(1920 - 1940 Daily)

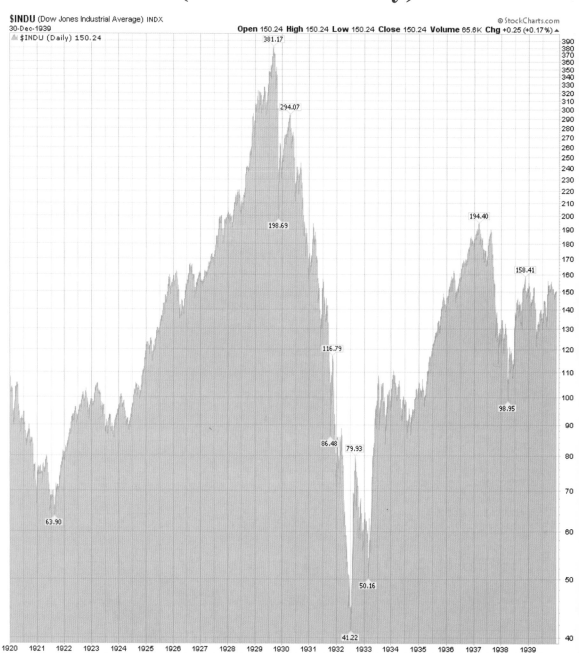

$INDU (Dow Jones Industrial Average) INDX
30-Dec-1939
Open 150.24 High 150.24 Low 150.24 Close 150.24 Volume 65.6K Chg +0.25 (+0.17%) ▲
© StockCharts.com
$INDU (Daily) 150.24

381.17
294.07
198.69
194.40
158.41
116.79
98.95
86.48
79.93
63.90
50.16
41.22

CHAPTER 3

Graph It Out!

Graphs measure data that change over time. The data are called **variables**. Some graphs use a grid made from two main lines. Each line is called an **axis**. The horizontal line is called the x-axis. The vertical line is called the y-axis. Graphs can compare more than one variable at once.

This line graphs shows that between 1920 and 1929, stock prices increased by 400 percent.

Line Graph

Entering data on a graph is called **plotting**. The location on the graph is called a **coordinate** point. Coordinate points are connected by a line.

A graph includes many parts:

Title: This tells a reader what the graph is about.

Legend: When a graph has more than one line, this tells what each line represents.

X-Axis: This shows the time period in units that the data covers.

Y-Axis: This shows the units used for measuring the data.

Data: This is the information being measured.

Line graphs are good for keeping track of how something increases or decreases over time.

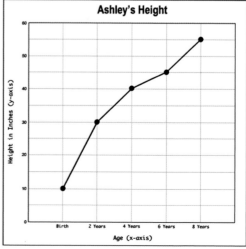

Try It!

Make a graph of your local weather over the period of a week.

1. On a sheet of notebook paper, copy the graph below. The degrees listed on your y-axis may need to start at a higher or lower temperature, depending on how warm it is outside. It does not need to start at zero. List temperatures by tens.

2. Check the temperature at the same time each day. You can either use a thermometer or check the temperature on a weather Web site.

3. Record your data at the point where the appropriate day and the temperature intersect on the graph.

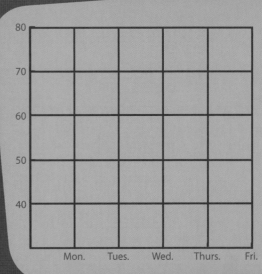

World Population by Continent

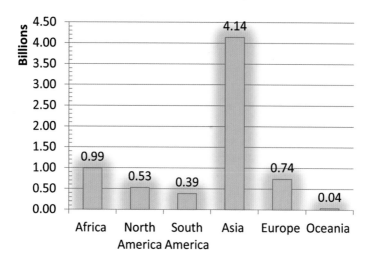

Bar graphs make it easy for people to see how different measurements compare to one another.

Bar Graphs

Like line graphs, bar graphs are useful for showing how the size of something changes over time. They are also good for comparing different groups of data. For example, a bar graph might be used to show a student's improvement in test scores. Or it could show changes in population. The most common bar graphs are vertical, but some are horizontal.

Try It!

Create a bar graph to compare the populations of Alaska, New Jersey, and Iowa. Here's how:

1. On a sheet of notebook paper, copy the graph below.
2. Visit the U.S. Census Bureau Population Finder Web site at *www.census.gov/popfinder/*. Find Alaska in the drop-down menu, and click "Display."
3. In Alaska's section, draw a bar that reaches the appropriate total population on the y-axis. Round the number to the nearest million.
4. Repeat steps 2 and 3 for the other two states.
5. Give your graph a title.

How does each state's population compare to other states?

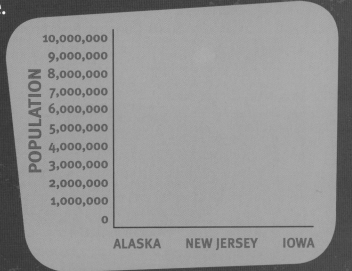

29

Pie Charts

Unlike line and bar graphs, circle graphs show percentages. Circle graphs are also known as pie charts because each section looks like a slice of pie. Each slice represents a fraction or percentage of the whole. The U.S. Census Bureau sometimes uses pie charts to show how many men versus women live in the United States. A pie chart can also show how the population is divided according to age or ethnic group.

Census statistics are often represented using circle graphs.

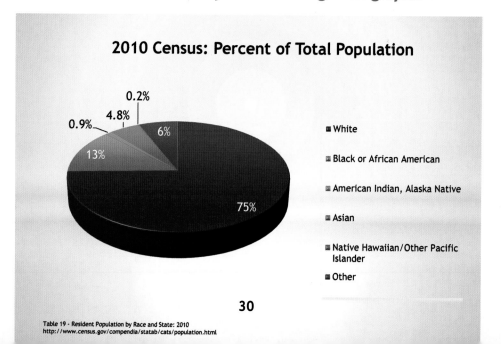

2010 Census: Percent of Total Population

- White
- Black or African American
- American Indian, Alaska Native
- Asian
- Native Hawaiian/Other Pacific Islander
- Other

0.2%
4.8%
0.9%
6%
13%
75%

Table 19 - Resident Population by Race and State: 2010
http://www.census.gov/compendia/statab/cats/population.html

Try It!

Create a pie chart showing your classmates' favorite hobbies. You might want to ask your teacher if you can do this as a class project. Follow these directions:

1. On a sheet of notebook paper, list three options, such as reading, video games, and sports.
2. Take a **poll**, asking each of your classmates to choose their favorite of the options.
3. For each hobby, divide the number of students who chose it by the total number of students. Multiply this number by 100 to find the percentage.
4. Draw a circle on a piece of notebook paper. Divide this chart into sections based on the percentage who chose each hobby.
5. Draw a legend to show what each section of the chart represents.

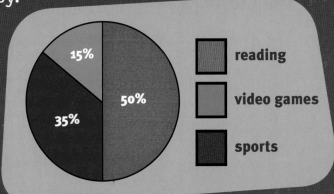

15%

50%

35%

reading

video games

sports

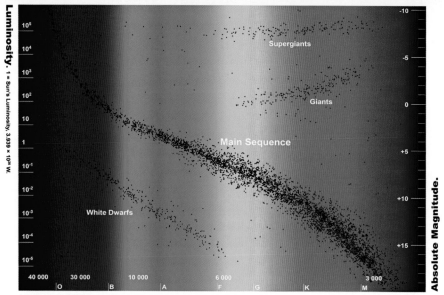

Luminosity. 1 = Sun's Luminosity. 3.939 × 10²⁶ W.

Absolute Magnitude.

Supergiants

Giants

Main Sequence

White Dwarfs

Spectral Class And Surface Temperature (K°).

Scientists use this scatter plot graph, called the Hertzprung-Russell Diagram, to study how stars' colors relate to how brightly they shine.

Scatter Plot Graphs

Data does not always follow a logical pattern. Scatter plots are useful for comparing more than one type of variable. Scientists use this graph to determine if there is a relationship between the data. If the data are close together, they are related. If the data are scattered all over the place, they are not. A line is sometimes drawn between the points to find an **average**.

Try It!

Create a scatter plot of your friends' and family members' birthdays. Try to use at least 10 people. Follow these directions:

1. Copy the chart below on a sheet of notebook paper.
2. Place a dot at the intersection of the month and date of each friend's birthday. What are the most common months? What are the most common days? Is there any relationship between months and days? Sometimes there is not.

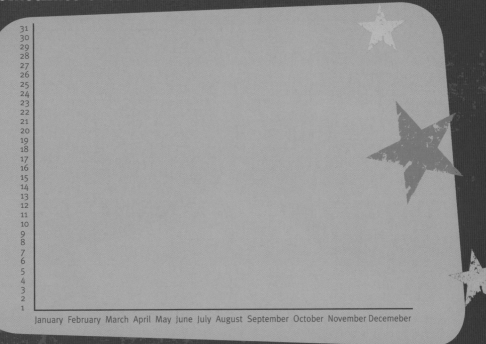

34

CHAPTER 4

Charts

Charts are a good way of showing information with words, pictures, or numbers. Charts in a classroom might show math facts, grammar rules, or even student progress. They can be used to show relationships between people, places, or things. Scientists, engineers, and businesses use charts to show data that does not change for a long time.

Sailors use charts to help navigate through large bodies of water.

Flowcharts

Flowcharts show how things or events are organized. They list each task in order. This is called a **sequence**. Engineers use flowcharts to list the sequence of steps needed to build something. Businesses use flowcharts to show the sequence of actions needed to make a decision. Flowcharts get their name because each task on a chart flows into another.

Construction workers use flowcharts to make sure they complete each part of a project in the right order.

36

Try It!

Create your own flowchart for an activity, such as baking cookies. Here's how:

1. Write down the steps that must take place to do the activity. What steps come first? Which come next? Some steps in a sequence do not depend on one another. Others can only work in a certain order. For example, you can gather ingredients before you turn on the oven. But you must turn on the oven before you are done mixing the ingredients so it will be hot enough when the dough is ready to bake.

2. Copy the steps into a flowchart, numbering each step in sequence.

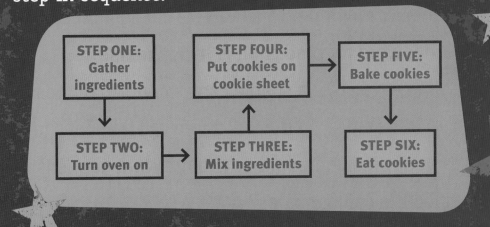

STEP ONE: Gather ingredients → STEP TWO: Turn oven on → STEP THREE: Mix ingredients → STEP FOUR: Put cookies on cookie sheet → STEP FIVE: Bake cookies → STEP SIX: Eat cookies

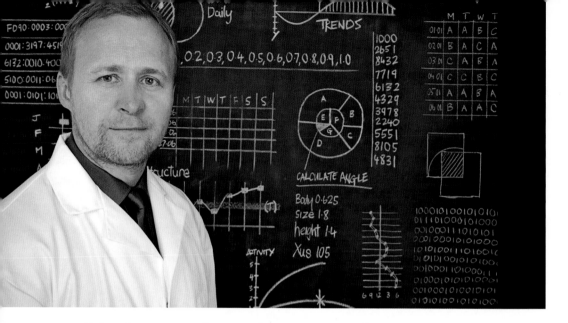

Scientists must often analyze very complicated data in order to predict the outcome of experiments.

Prediction Charts

Scientists conduct experiments to find the answer to a question. They use their knowledge to guess what the answer might be. This guess is called a prediction. Another word for prediction is **hypothesis**. Try creating a chart for a simple experiment: a coin toss. On what side do you think the coin will fall? Try again. Was your prediction right or wrong? What happens if you flip the coin 20 times?

Try It!

Prediction charts are useful for other projects, too. When you read a book, do you try to predict what will happen next? A prediction chart is a good way of making notes and reviewing what you've read. Here's how you can use one:

1. Copy the chart below on a piece of notebook paper.
2. Write down predictions about a book you are reading.
3. When you've finished the book, compare your predictions to the book's real ending. Were you correct?

My Prediction	Why I Made This Prediciton	Was My Prediction Correct?	
		Yes	No

Character-Traits Charts

Authors often make charts to keep track of character-traits. A trait describes the way a character looks, talks, or feels. A character-traits chart helps an author remember which character has brown eyes and which has green ones. The chart might show how a character reacts to a problem. Is the character timid or brave when danger is near?

NAME _____ DATE _____

Character-Traits Chart

Character's Name	Describe the Character	Analyze the Character and His or Her Actions

The most characters given individual voices in an audio book is 224, in George R. R. Martin's A Game of Thrones.

A character-traits chart can be very helpful if you are writing a story.

The Family Tree

Genealogy is the study of families and their ancestors. One way of recording this information is to create a chart. The chart shows how each member of a family is related to another. The diagram is called a family tree because of its shape. Each part of a family branches out to connect to new family members.

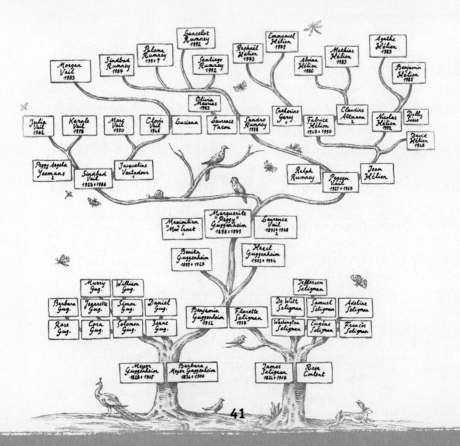

Note-Taking Organizer

MY NOTES

Main points from my notes

1. _____
_____
2. _____
_____
3. _____
_____

Two questions I still have

1. _____
_____
2. _____
_____

Strategies that I will use to answer my questions.
_____
_____
_____
_____
_____
_____

Organized notes are much easier to use than sloppy ones.

Note-Taking Charts

Charts can be used to make notes about questions you have. They can be used when taking notes in class, while planning a project, or when brainstorming an idea. Try using this note-taking chart when studying for an assignment. What are the subject's main points? What questions do you have? Where can you go to find the answers?

Organization for Any Occasion

There are countless varieties of charts and graphs from which to choose. If you cannot find the perfect one for your task, you can adapt one to fit. Whether you are comparing data, tracking variables, taking a poll, or just trying to decide what food to order, a graphic organizer can help you out. ★

The right chart can make any task simpler.

True Statistics

Number of people in the world: 7 billion, as of 2012

Number of people in the United States: 313 million, as of 2012

Number of U.S. accountants and auditors in 2008: 1.3 million

Average U.S. family size in 2010: 2.59

Total number of passengers flying through the United States in 2010: 786.7 million

Number of available rows in an Excel spreadsheet as of 2012: More than 1 million

Year the periodic table was first developed: 1869, by Dmitry Mendeleyev

Age of the oldest known lunar calendar: 15,000 years

Did you find the truth?

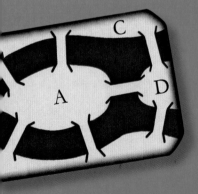

F Spreadsheets were tablecloths used by tax collectors to count the king's money.

T The oldest known Mayan calendar shows dates as far as 7012 CE.

Resources

Books

Dowdy, Penny. *Graphing*. New York: Crabtree Publishing, 2008.

Piddock, Claire. *Line, Bar, and Circle Graphs*. New York: Crabtree Publishing, 2010.

Priestley, Michael. *Charts, Tables, and Graphs*. New York: Teaching Resources, 2005.

Taylor-Butler, Christine. *Understanding Diagrams*. New York: Children's Press, 2013.

Visit this Scholastic Web site for more information on understanding charts and graphs:
www.factsfornow.scholastic.com
★ Enter the keywords **Charts and Graphs**

Important Words

average (AV-ur-ij) — a number that you get by adding a group of numbers together and then dividing the sum by the number of figures you have added

axis (AK-sis) — a line at the side or the bottom of a graph

coordinate (koh-OR-duh-nit) — describing all or part of a set of numbers used to show the position of a point on a line, graph, or map

credits (KRED-its) — records of money that is added to an account

debits (DEB-its) — records of money that is taken out of an account

hypothesis (hye-PAH-thi-sis) — an idea that could explain how something works but that has to be tested through experiments to be proven

intersect (in-tur-SEKT) — to meet or cross something

nodes (NOHDZ) — points at which lines or pathways intersect

plotting (PLAHT-ing) — marking out something based on calculations

poll (POHL) — a survey of people's opinions or beliefs

sequence (SEE-kwuhns) — a series or collection of things that follow each other in a particular order

variables (VAIR-ee-uh-buhlz) — data that change over time

Index

Page numbers in **bold** indicate illustrations

About the Author

Christine Taylor-Butler is the author of more than 60 books for children, including the True Book series on American History/ Government, Health and the Human Body, and Science Experiments. A graduate of the Massachusetts Institute of Technology, Christine holds degrees in both civil engineering and art and design. She currently lives in Kansas City, Missouri.

M6

11-12